LIGHT THROUGH THE CRACKS

FROM BROKENNESS TO ROYALTY – A WOMAN'S JOURNEY TO DIVINE IDENTITY

Dr. Cheryl Kehl

DEDICATION

THIS BOOK IS DEDICATED TO ALL THE WOMEN WHO HAVE STAYED IN PLACES LONGER THAN GOD INTENDED. I PRAY THIS BOOK GIVES YOU THE COURAGE TO IDENTIFY YOUR PURPOSE, AND GET OUT OF THE DRY AND UNFRUITFUL PLACES IN YOUR LIFE. YOU ARE THE DAUGHTER OF THE KING. CLAIM YOUR CROWN.

Table of Contents

This page is left blank intentionally

Introduction

This is what I prayer-fully ask this book will touch the lives of many women who are or have walked through the fires of life and feel like God has forgotten you. He is waiting and ready to restore you and crown you as the queen He intended you to be. This book is dedicated to the women who need to know that God can use broken vessels and He wants to show you how much He loves you.

I wrote the below monologue when I entered the 2025 Ms. Senior Jacksonville pageant. I cannot sing, I cannot dance, and did not know what I would do for my talent. Little did I know that this was something God gave me that would go way beyond the pageant and be the beginning of a ministry where He could begin to heal the wounds of women around the world. The talent portion was only two minutes. Those two minutes opened some doors but I felt He has a greater work He wanted to do so that is why this book was birthed.

The Crack in the Crown

I was born a secret,
A whisper my father barely spoke of.
Labelled a mistake, but heavenly called me chosen.
Raised in the shadows, but I was never out of the sight of
God.

Love came dressed as lies,
With fist that claimed they cared.
Marriage after marriage they tried to break me.
But the breaking, was the birthing of my becoming,
Then God sent me my king.

Life tried to shut me up,
Steal my voice, Snatch my worth, Silence my praise.
But God,
God saw purpose in my pain.
And the cracks they left behind, that is where His light
began to shine through.

I'm not just alive, I'm alive in Him.
Breathing purpose,
Walking in power,
Wearing life's storms like a badge of honor.

I didn't just come through,
I came through blazing.

Not because it was easy,
But because I didn't quit!

So, Sis if life has you feeling cracked, battered or bruised.
Don't you dare believe that you are broken beyond repair.
Because it's in your cracks that God's glory will shine
through.

This is what redemption looks like,
Empowered...Walking in Greatness.. & Shining bright for
the world to see.

CHAPTER 1

Born a Secret

I was born a secret child of my father. After my mother had gotten pregnant she found out that he was a married man with two children. So my father's immediate family member's kept me a secret. I was only able to meet a handful of family members which included his parents, my uncles, brothers and his ex-wife after her finding out about me and the divorce. There was no big baby shower welcoming the new baby to the family. I was the child that was kept in the shadows and brought out only at planned and specific times. This experience left me wondering where I fit in the world or even in my family.

Because I grew up thinking my real identity was a secret it reflected negatively on my self-esteem. Being an invisible child caused me to want to do a lot of things alone. My mother soon decided after having another child by another man who was not her husband that she wanted to give us to our grandparents to raise. This in my eyes was just another act of rejection by a parent. There has always been an absence of affirmation in my life as a child. And even as an adult for that matters from my parents. The void of a missing a father and mother left a hole in my soul.

One hard thing I learned as a child was that I always felt like I needed to perform and fake as if I was happy. I had to continue through life with a smile even though I had a very heavy heart. I learned how to make it appear that I was ok even though I felt like my life was a lie. This was extremely hard to do as a child trying to find my way in life. Being hidden affects your self-perception. I felt like a shadow and didn't really think I had a real life. Furthermore, I sunk deeper into the shadow of silence as the years went on. Shadows seemed to have no place anywhere and remain hidden from the light.

I got really good at acting and swore one day I would land a leading role in a movie or television show. I learned to act like I didn't care about anything. I acted like I was not hurting deep in my soul every day; acted like I really didn't know what was going on with my family situation; acted like being excluded didn't bother me. But, it did. Every, Single Day Of My Life.

As I got older, the walls kept building to keep people out - but it also kept me trapped inside. I longed to be chosen, to be claimed, to be called a beloved daughter -

not just by blood but by love. Identity is fragile when it's based on the absence of others.

Shame crept in and told me so many lies. That I wasn't worth claiming or showing up for. That I was unworthy of love. That I would never be more than a secret. But the devil is a liar. And one day God interrupted those lies, with truth so powerful it shattered the silence I had lived in for years.

Psalms 27:10 became my lifeline: "Though my father and my mother forsake me; then the Lord will receive me." I read it once, I read it twice, then again and again, until the words stopped being ink on paper and became the anchor of my soul.

God received me not as a mistake but as a chosen vessel and beloved daughter of His. I began to see myself as His masterpiece. God knew from the beginning how I was going to be conceived and brought into this world and He didn't think less of me. Because of everything I have gone through, the call God has placed on my life became more significant.

Somewhere around the time I turned 50 years old. I no longer wanted to have a secret relationship with my father. My demand was that he would publicly acknowledge me or we would go our separate ways. To my disappointment we went our separate ways. God then showed me I was a sign and not a secret. A sign that He sees. A sign that He heals. A sign that even though I was abandoned He still placed an anointing on my life.

If this chapter speaks to you hear me clearly; you my sister or brother... you are not a secret. You became the story that God is still writing. Just like me, the world is waiting and needing to hear your story of redemption.

Reflection

"Though my father and mother forsake me, the Lord will receive me." - Psalm 27:10

In this chapter we are reminded that who we walk with defines our trip, not where we started. This is important for you to understand. This chapter illustrates how suffering can be transformed into meaning, serving as a reminder that God is always there, even when we are at our lowest. God's hand has always been leading us, whether it is concealed, wounded or mended.

Even though we may experience heartbreaking situations in life, the Bible teaches us that we are not alone. God accepts us while the world rejects us. His truth becomes our song when trauma steals our voice. When we put our wounds in His hands, they become our insight.

Today reflect on your journey through the lens of redemption. Let the above scripture anchor your heart and build your faith. Because God doesn't just heal – He crowns. He doesn't just restore – He reveals. He is not done with you yet. Just yield to Him. And watch how He uses you to bring healing to those assigned to you.

CHAPTER 2

Love That Hurts

I remember thinking love is not supposed to hurt like this. I remember seeing how in love my godparents were and how their marriage seemed to be so perfect. I always wondered early on in marriage why I could not experience this type of love. I never had physical bruises to show because he never hit me in the face or anything. But boy, did we fight! And I always fought back as hard as I could. I fought like my life depended on it and it did. That is the reason I always believe I survived and got out as soon as I did. For many of us women love came with wounds, instead of love and warmth. All those broken promises turned into pain, and home became a place we had to tiptoe through like a minefield.

When I was eleven years old, I remember looking through bridal magazines and planning what I thought would be the perfect wedding and marriage. Now looking back did I really believe in fairy tales like that? Yes, I did watching all those movies had my head dreaming of a fairytale wedding. I did have a lot of hopes early in my life that love would find me and fix me somehow. I believed whole heartly that if I gave enough, forgave enough – they would change. I found that the cycle of domestic violence is subtle at first. But it grows progressively and builds fast.

It sometimes begins simply as verbal abuse. It then may progress to a slap, push or punch. To the abuser, it is all about control & power and nothing more. They begin to find ways to isolate you so that your friends and family do not see what is going on. They speak words that chip away at who you are until you forget that you're worthy of a better life.

My first abuser grew up in a home where his mother was abused on a daily basis. So he thought that it was a normal way of life. He knew that I did not have a huge amount of self-esteem because of what I had been through and used that to his advantage. But what he did not realize was that where I drew the line was him putting his hands on me. That was more than I was willing to take because I had not grown up that way. He thought me fighting back was crazy and that I would get tired and give in. But that did not happen. I was able to get out because we were living on a military installation and I saw a counselor two times a month. I told my counselor one day that I would lay awake at night thinking about how I could kill him and not go to jail. That was all she needed to hear and had me out of the house in one hour and on my way to a battered woman's shelter.

Some of the women I met while in the shelter had stories that were unbelievable to me. I heard women saying that they had been taking beatings for many years. They would all say that they believed somehow it was their fault. I did not understand that at first but after talking to more and more women, my eyes were open to the cycle of domestic violence. The cycle of abuse can make you numb; the abuser plays with your mind and makes you feel like you are to blame. Deep down inside, these women wanted to be rescued and after a while they got the courage to escape. The sad thing is I saw many return back. This was because they did not think they could support themselves and children.

I fell into the trap of false hope which is dangerous and that is why I stayed as long as I did. False hope makes women hear the apologies from the abuser as a turning point. They sometimes stay not because they don't want better – but because they believe that maybe this time it will be different. Every single time they find out this time is no different than the last time. Each time a piece of them disappears in the lie.

I found that I stayed in places too long where God never called me to. I begin to see that I confused loyalty with bondage. I realized at some point that God is not the author of confusion or chaos, this is what helped open my eyes. His love isn't controlling. His love isn't violent. His love is not abusive. So that is not the life that He wanted for me or for you.

When the counselor talked me into to leaving so quickly, it was not easy for me to leave. I didn't have a job or a car so I had no money. I had 3 kids and was pregnant with my 4th child. Leaving came with fear and judgment from friends. But it also came with freedom. I felt at peace by the next morning. The peace wasn't from the absence of a man it was peace from the presence of God.

God's love met me at the shelter. His love didn't demand an explanation. It didn't make false excuses. His love held me. God began to restore every part of me that was torn down. If you are in a place that is breaking you, let this be your sign. God is calling you out – not into loneliness, but into liberty.

Reflection

'He has sent me to bind up the brokenhearted...' - Isaiah 61:1

This chapter paints a picture of pain turned into purpose, reminding us that God's presence is unwavering, even in our lowest moments. Whether hidden, hurt, or healing, God's hand has always been guiding us and will save us.

Life's crushing moments may try to break us, but the Word of God reassures us that we are not abandoned. When the world rejects us, God receives us. When our voice is stolen by trauma, His truth becomes our song. Every wound we carry becomes a wellspring of wisdom when placed in His hands He loves us unconditionally.

We may start as survivors, but with God, we become signposts of His grace. Our scars tell stories of victory, our silence becomes strength, and our brokenness reveals His beauty. Embrace the divine truth that you are not just surviving—you are being shaped for significance. You are royalty, not because of the world's affirmation, but because of your divine adoption into His Kingdom.

Today, reflect on your journey through the lens of redemption. Let the scripture anchor your heart and stir up faith. Because God doesn't just heal—He crowns. He doesn't just restore—He reveals. And He is not finished with you yet.

CHAPTER 3

Love Dressed as Lies

As I mentioned in the last chapter, at eleven I would dream up my wedding day. I planned what I thought would be reality for me. I thought marriage would be the stairwell to my stability and protection. And love that lasted and stayed forever. But I soon found that in my life love was chains of bondage and fists that really didn't care where they landed.

My first marriage was at the tender age of 19 because I was pregnant with my 1st child. It started with promises that he was going to take care of us and that life was going to be great. The marriage was not physically abusive but he became so caught up in drinking and getting high that he could not keep a job. He then began to just lounge around the house. We had to move in with my mother due to finances. I came up with the ideal that I would join the Navy so that we could move out of my mother's home and live a real family life. But after finishing bootcamp and moving to Florida and getting my own place, my plans changed. I thought if I had to do it alone, I would do it alone, because my husband said he was not going to work when he got to Florida: he would just stay home and take care of the girls. I thought with all the drinking and drugging, he could not take care of himself never mind take care of my girls. So, I left him in New Jersey where he was.

The Navy was where I met my 2nd husband: the abuser. This is when I found myself dealing with the pain of emotional manipulation and someone who was full of lies. Because it was my 2nd failed attempt at marriage, I stayed way too long and dealt with way too much. At one point he had myself and 2 other women pregnant at the same time. I stayed and called it love but it was really survival. I called it commitment but it was really captivity.

So, by the time I escaped this cycle, I was worn thin. As stated before, this marriage ended with a lot of fighting and shame. After getting through all of this I felt like I needed to return to the God I knew as a teenager. Before we split up my husband received orders to a base in New Jersey so we packed up and left Florida. So, after leaving the shelter I moved to back to where my family lived and found a church and started attending. Now, I was single again with four kids. I became what I now know to be as a "target" to an older gentleman in the church. I say this because I later learned his thoughts was "she has all these kids she must love having sex." We started dating and once again I became pregnant this time with my 5th child. We got married and life was good for a little while. I loved Florida so much I wanted to move my new family back to the sunshine state. So I applied for a job at Prudential Insurance company and moved my family.

Somewhere about 5 years into this 3rd marriage my ex-husband developed water on the brain which I found out long after it happened that this caused most of our problems. He was not in his right mind and became extremely verbally abusive to the point I had to obtain a restraining order and file for divorce. He was removed from the home and within a couple weeks he moved back to New Jersey. It was about a year later I found out about the water on the brain. He passed away from some complication about 6 months after the discovery.

I started evaluating where my life had gone wrong so many times. One thing I discovered was that I was looking for a person to erase all of my pain. This never happened it the pain only multiplied. I realized that each wedding ring came with new vows, but the same patterns of abuse and unhappiness. That was because I kept bringing the same broken and unhappy woman into the mix of things. Each man thought that he was promising me forever but they could not handle the scars I carried. I soon found the answer I needed and took my brokenness to God. He was the only man that could help me. I was too broken for the other people to deal with.

My good Father God came along and with His mercy and love, I was not too broken for Him to love me. God began to gently and lovingly unravel the layers that I had wrapped around my identity. He began to show me that His covenant doesn't resemble man's broken promises. God revealed to me that love isn't meant to leave you bleeding. Love doesn't have to silence your soul to protect someone else's image or selfishness. This is when I really started to discover what real love felt like.

As I begin to heal and mature, I had to grieve for the girl who thought marriage would fix her. I had to see that I was expecting someone else to make me happy. That was a huge responsibility I put on other people and that was not fair. I am responsible for my own happiness. I had to forgive myself for the bad choices I made in life. I had to sit with God and have Him redefine what love looks like – through His word and not through my wounds. This was not easy but was so worth it.

The more I accepted the truth of God's love, the less I could stand the fake love. I began to realize that my worth wasn't based on what I could do for a man, but on who I was to my maker. I learned that it was better for me to be whole and alone than to be broken and tied to bondage. After healing from my previous trauma. God sent me the husband that loves and cherishes me. We do not have a perfect marriage but because we both love God we work hard on keeping our marriage together and loving each other.

Reflection

"Love is patient, love is kind. It does not envy, it does not boast, it is not proud... It does not dishonor others, it is not self-seeking, it is not easily angered, it keeps no record of wrongs." —1 Corinthians 13:4-5

There is a hurt that whispers rather than screams. It appears as love, but below it lies confusion, power, and betrayal. Since the person who held you close is also the one who crushed your spirit, "love dressed as lies" is a difficult reality to confront. Admitting that something that was meant to protect you has actually pierced you is difficult. The very hands that had previously clasped each other ended up getting bruised. Those lips that said "I love you" also spoke things that made you feel less valuable.

Since it distorts the meaning of love, this type of deception is the most severe hurt. It skews trust. Additionally, it causes you to doubt not only other people but also yourself. "Did I cause it?" "Did I overlook the indicators?" "What kept me here for so long?" What could I have done differently? I didn't know if it was all my fault or if there was someone else was the blame.

But listen, dear: You weren't harmed by love. It was love disguised as manipulation. Furthermore, God never created a love that leaves you speechless and broken. According to 1 Corinthians 13, love is compassionate, patient, intolerant of rage, and devoid of dishonor. A counterfeit love was what I was experiencing and it didn't fit God's concept of true love.

God heals when love hurts. God becomes our haven when we lose trust. "The Lord is near to the brokenhearted and saves those who are crushed in spirit," according to Psalm 34:18. He enters your pain rather than avoiding it. He whispers, "You are worthy," and envelops you like a real father. He loves you deeply.

After falsehoods, there is life. After confusion, there is clarity. Real love, on the other hand, is the type that doesn't bruise, control, or silence. A real man gave His life in order to save you. Jesus is his name. He creates new hearts, not merely repairs shattered ones.

The fake love you experienced does not define you. The true love that saved you defines who you are. Allow God to redefine what love means in your life. Learn from Him what it means to be loved, respected, and esteemed—not just by other people, but also by the person who knows you the best. That person is the One who created you.

So let the falsehood go today. Take back the truth. Additionally, keep in mind that crying does not imply weakness. You are stronger than you realize you can endure it and come out on the other side.

CHAPTER 4

Silenced but Still Standing

There is a certain silence that arises from suffering rather than from tranquility. I didn't suddenly lose my voice, it was broken up over the years. As time went on, I discovered that being silent protected me, and silence became my survival. I was free to talk, I had big dreams once. However, I was shut down when my presence had to become a performance and love turned into danger. I told myself that keeping quiet was preferable to running the risk of being rejected yet again. I thought it was better to pretend than to fail again.

But God was speaking even in the quiet. He was whispering bravery in the silence of my terror. He was planting strength in the echoes of my uncertainty. After so many failures it paralyzes you on your next move. One prayer, one cry, one breath at a time. God was rebuilding my voice, even though I was unaware at the time. Silence, I believed, was a sign of weakness. However, I've discovered that some of the most powerful conflicts are waged in silence. No one hears the prayers whispered through tears in worship; in the choice to get up one more time when it would be simpler to stop.

I started writing initially in journals and later in letters to God. When my lips were still shaking, I spoke with my pen. I want to encourage you to just start writing even if it's in a notebook or journal. Strength gradually returned to me, not loud, not dazzling however, it was rooted. Actual. Redeemed.

God just asks for truth; He never asked me to speak loudly. And He responded to my broken whispers with a shout. A shout of authority rather than rage. Not with resentment but with courage. He reminded me that when a woman belongs to Him, she is still courageous even when she is silent. I stand now because grace got me back up when I was knocked down. God never sat down on me, which is why I'm still standing today.

I want you to know that God can still hear you even when can you no longer speak due to the pain. Your quiet doesn't frighten Him. Your suffering does not drive Him away. He draws near to the broken hearted. And He is prepared to restore your voice, not only to talk but to declare His goodness in your life.

God is restoring you even now. You're still upright. You'll soon be able to speak once more with authority, truth, and the strength of a woman who has persevered through the stillness and returned stronger. Because when God gives you your voice back, it doesn't come back soft. It comes back like a trumpet declaring I'm still here. I still matter. And I still belong to the King.

Reflection

"We are hard pressed on every side, but not crushed..." In this chapter we were reminded that who we walk with defines our trip, not where we started. This chapter illustrates how suffering can be transformed into meaning, serving as a reminder that God is always there, even we are at our lowest. God's hand is always leading us, whether it is concealed, wounded, or mending. - 2 Corinthians 4:8-9

Even though we may experience heartbreaking situations in our life, the Bible teaches us that we are not alone. God fully accepts us while the world rejects us. His truth becomes our song when trauma steals our voice. When we put our wounds in His hands, they become a source of light for us and others.

Even though we begin as survivors. God uses us to spread His grace. Our brokenness shows His beauty, our silence becomes strength, and our wounds tell tales of triumph. Accept the divine reality that you are being molded for meaning rather than merely existing. You are royalty because of your supernatural adoption into the Kingdom, not because of approval from the outside world.

Consider your journey through the prism of redemption today. Allow the scripture to bolster your faith and serve as an anchor, because God crowns, not just heals. He discloses rather than merely restores.

CHAPTER 5

The Crack is Where God's Light Shines Through

I once believed that in order to be used by God, I had to be whole and have a perfect life. I thought I needed to be flawless. However, God uses broken things to accomplish His best work. And I didn't realize how much He wanted to shine through me until I was broken.

We spend a lot of time attempting to conceal our flaws by masking them with silence, smiles, and makeup. But concealing gets in the way of healing. It's in the sunshine that healing occurs. Additionally, if there are no cracks, light cannot enter in. This fact was so freeing for me. I begin to welcome the cracks in my life. This gave a place for me to see God's light.

The shame I carried told me my story was too messy to matter. That I should just pretend that everything was ok. But something else was whispered by God; "Let me use what they attempted to break." He said, "permit me to use the broken parts. Wow, that was so profound to me and I had to let Him use the parts" to see how He could change lives.

The Japanese have an art form called kintsugi – which means "golden journey". They do not discard ceramic bowls that break. Thery use gold to fix it. Additionally the cracks become part of the design making it more valuable and attractive than before.

That's what God does with us. He doesn't erase our brokenness. He fills it with glory, with grace, with His spirit. And the place we thought disqualified us becomes the very places He uses to minister to others.

My life is no longer a secret. I know longer hide my scars, since they are all testimonies. Every crack serves evidence that I have lived. I recovered. I'm still here. And I'm thriving, not simply surviving. Because of the cracks, not despite them.

The enemy wanted me to feel ashamed of my brokenness. God intended for it to mold me. I now see purpose rather than suffering when I reflect on my past and the pain. From hopelessness to destiny, I see a path of grace.

To every woman reading this – stop trying to get yourself together in secret. Bring your fragments to God. Allow Him to pour gold into you. Allow Him to transform what you believe to be ruined into something lovely. You are not irreparably damaged. You are an honorable vessel. A work of art in process. What are your cracks? It is through them the light enters and His majesty is revealed.

So don't curse the cracks. Celebrate them. Because it is evidence that you were broken, yes – but you didn't stay that way. You were rebuilt by the hands of the Master, and you shine with the glory of the One who will never let you go.

Reflection

"But we have this treasure in jars of clay to show that this all-surpassing power is from God and not from us." — 2 Corinthians 4:7

Some breaks includes broken relationships, abuse, and abandonment are loud and noticeable. Others take place in the shadowy recesses of our psyche, where guilt and secrets fester. The fact that breaking is not the end of the tale is true regardless of how we break. It might even be the beginning of the true story of your life right now.

The sacred picture of broken pottery filled with light—the fissures, the scars, the very places we formerly wished to conceal—is the foundation of this thought. These fractures and wounds become channels for God's beauty.

The enemy's lie is, "You're too broken to be useful." But the truth is that the flaws make you useful. They are where kindness flows. They are the places where empathy resides. They let God's light out and help other people find their path in the dark. This is so powerful.

Your tale, which is about heartbreak and healing, is a light. Your journey is more than just surviving; it's a signal fire telling other women, "You're not alone, and you're not too far gone."

CHAPTER 6

Alive in Him

There came a time in my life when I realized I was not just alive – but I was alive in Him. Every breath, every heartbeat, every step forward was no longer fueled by fear or shame. It was driven by the power of the One who brought me back from the edge.

Jesus did more than save me from the abyss. He purposely brought me back to life. He offered me a new tune in addition to calming the storm. I previously lived with wounds and questioned whether I would ever fully recover. However, I now live as a real example of how mercy is stronger than every error and grace is greater than sorrow.

I don't just exist. I don't merely survive. I live completely profoundly, consciously, because I'm alive in Him with the same spirit that raised Jesus from the dead. And that power didn't come to make me comfortable in my mess. I became brave as a result of His spirit in me. I look for challenges and ways to come out of my comfort zone. This helps me to keep soaring higher. Not for me but to show other women that they can do whatever they put their mind to do.

And I refuse to apologize for the light in me. I refuse to dim down to make others comfortable. Because I know what it has costs me to glow like this. I fought hell and live to worship my heavenly Father for all He has brought me through. I have wept many lonely nights and now I am walking in the morning joy of Jesus.

Living with purpose is what it means to be alive in Christ. It is to walk with your spirit burning brightly, your scars healed, and your head held high. It's to know that whatever God has infused into you will always come back, regardless of who departed or what was lost.

You, my sister, were never meant to barely make it, you were meant to flourish and thrive, to take the lead and to be radiant and shine bright for the world to see. The same power that carried you through will continue bringing you forward. You are alive in Him, So walk like it. Live like it. Because when He lives in you, defeat is never your final chapter. Nothing can silence a woman who knows her savior lives in her.

Reflection

"I have been crucified with Christ and I no longer live, but Christ lives in me. The life I now live in the body, I live by faith in the Son of God, who loved me and gave himself for me." — Galatians 2:20

Being "alive in Him" doesn't mean that everything is flawless. It doesn't mean that I never feel pain or think about the past. It means that even if those things are still going on, they don't define me anymore. I used to think that those who injured me or what I've been through defined me, but now that I know who He is and what He did for me on the cross defines me and who I will always be.

Galatians 2:20 is not merely a verse to remember; it is a statement of resurrection. It states, "I am not the woman who was used, abused, left, or embarrassed." That part of me was buried with Christ. And now, every step I take and every breath I take is proof that Christ lives in me.

That kind of awakening has power. The enemy is afraid of a woman who has been harmed; he is afraid of a woman who has healed. He is afraid of the woman who knows how much she is worth to Christ and lives that way. He is afraid of the lady who brings light where there was previously darkness, since that kind of woman is a threat to hell.

CHAPTER 7

The Crown after the Crushing

There's a crushing that comes before the crown. Before the glory, there's the grief. Before the honor, there's the heartbreak. And before you walk in victory, you crawl through the valley.

It wasn't easy for me to get here. My crown was created in a fire, not given to me. You ask, "is it a crown from the pageant you were in?" My answer is "no, it is a crown of grace, given by God as being the daughter of a King." It was formed in the midnight hours when tears were my only prayer. It was rooted in the soul of survival, cultivated by loss, and molded by betrayal. You may see the joy and strength now. But you didn't see the nights I wept uncontrollably, praying for God to just let me wake up whole. You didn't hear the whispers that told me I was unlovable, forgotten, and worthless.

The crushing didn't come to kill me. It came to anoint me. Like the olive crushed for its oil, the process was painful, but the results powerful. Power to stand. Power to speak. Power to wear a crown not of arrogance, but of authority.

God did. He noticed. He listened. And He got involved in my pain, rather that dismissing it. I turned to Him as a hiding place. My refuge, my safe place, and my source. He started to raise me up – not to be myself again, but to crown me into the person I was destined to be in Him.

To us, royalty is the epitome of perfection. However, true royalty appears as tenacity. It's the woman who, despite being broken, never gives up, never fails to show up, and never stops loving others. The father (God) who claimed me as His own, gave me a crown, not man. It's not something you have to earn. You don't need to pretend. Heaven's approval of you and not public acclaim, is the foundation of your crown. No one can take that away from you. You are royalty because God declared it.

The crushing seasons served as preparation rather than

punishment. I wasn't being broken down by God to be left empty, but in order for what remained to bear the weight of His calling, He was shattering what had to go.

Not because I've never felt down, but because I know the one who raised me up, I now walk with my head held high. Even though the public cannot see my crown, I can sense it. I have it with me. I'm a living example. And every action I take serves as evidence that while I have been crushed, I have also been crowned.

Reflection

'Now there is in store for me the crown of righteousness...'
- 2 Timothy 4:8

We are reminded that who we walk with defines our trip, not where we started. This chapter illustrates how suffering can be transformed into meaning, serving as a reminder that God is always there, even when we are at our lowest. God's hand has always been leading us, whether it is concealed, wounded, or mending He is there.

Even though we may experience heartbreaking situations in life, the Bible teaches us that we are not alone. God accepts us while the world rejects us. His truth becomes our song when trauma steals our voice. When we put our wounds in His hands, they become a source of insight.

Even though we begin as survivors, God uses us to spread

His grace. Our brokenness shows His beauty, our silence becomes strength, and our wounds tell tales of triumph. Accept the divine reality that you are being molded for meaning rather than merely existing. You are royalty because of your supernatural adoption into the Kingdom, not because of approval from the outside world.

Consider your journey through the prism of redemption today. Allow the scripture to bolster your faith and serve as an anchor. Because God crowns, not just heals. He discloses rather than merely restores. Furthermore, He is not yet done with you.

CHAPTER 8

Breaking the Silence for Others

I never imagined that what I thought of as my silence would end up saving someone else's life, that another woman's story would be infused with my scars. However, God starts using you as soon as He starts healing you.

I was ashamed to discuss my experiences in the beginning, because I thought people would judge me. I also thought that no one would believe me, because everything was done in the dark. I kept everything that was happening to me stored in a vault of shame. God has a way of making the very thing we conceal into the thing He emphasizes.

You see, the enemy thrives in your silence. He hopes our

shame will shut us down. But when we speak our truth it loosens his grip. When we testify, we knock down walls. Every time we say "me too," we are throwing lifelines to someone who thought they were drowning alone.

I came to see that my recovery was about more than just me. It had to do with the generations that would follow me. Looking for a sign that they can get better. That sign became me. I'm proof that God redeems, not because I'm flawless. I started to guide, coach, and support other women; I began to write, pray, and make room for stories that needed to be told. Not everything was as simple as it sounds. However, it was sacred. Whenever a woman said "thank you for speaking" I realized I was walking in my divine calling.

We all have a story to tell. And if you've made it through anything, you have a responsibility to speak not from a place of pride, but from a place of power. Your story is someone else's key to freedom. God didn't heal me to keep me quiet. He healed me so that I could proclaim His goodness. He gave me beauty for ashes so that I could show others that beauty still blooms in broken places.

If you are wondering whether to speak but are afraid – do it afraid. Because someone else is waiting for you to have the confidence to give them theirs. Now, I no longer hide my past. I say go. I declare, not whisper. Because I've discovered meaning in speaking up. I've also helped others find their voice by sharing my story.

Reflection

'They triumphed over him by the blood of the Lamb and by the word of their testimony." - Revelation 12:11

In this chapter we are reminded that our journey is not defined by where we began but by who walks with us. This chapter paints a picture of pain turned into purpose, reminding us that God's presence is unwavering, even in our lowest moments. Whether hidden, hurt, or healing, God's hand has always been guiding us through it all.

Life's crushing moments may try to break us, but the Word of God reassures us that we are not abandoned. When the world rejects us, God receives us. When our voice is stolen by trauma, His truth becomes our song. Every wound we carry becomes a wellspring of wisdom when placed in His hands. So don't be afraid to give it to Him.

We may start as survivors, but with God, we become signposts of His grace. Our scars tell stories of victory, our silence becomes strength, and our brokenness reveals His beauty. Embrace the divine truth that you are not just surviving—you are being shaped for significance. You are royalty, not because of the world's affirmation, but because of your divine adoption into the Kingdom.

Today, reflect on your journey through the lens of redemption. Let the scripture anchor your heart and stir up faith. Because God doesn't just heal—He crowns. He doesn't just restore—He reveals.

CHAPTER 9

Royal Reflections

Until we take a moment to reflect, we may not fully appreciate how far we have come. I hardly know the girl I use to be, the one who was stifled by fear, buried under shame, and burdened by secrets. I remembers a time not being able to look people in the eye. I was afraid, I was obscured. I wasn't even aware of the parts where I was broken. Even if I didn't feel it, I was brave. Because I continued. I kept waking up, praying through the pain, trusting through the tears.

The journey to royalty isn't straight. It's winding and wild. It comes with detours, and deep disappointments. But every step was a lesson. Every fall was a set-up, for a rise up. Every tear watered the seeds of my future.

I have no regrets about the journey. Not the gloomy

evenings. Not the roads that were broken, since they guided me to my Savior's feet. The actual healing started when they got me to my knees. He then raised me up to shine, not merely to stand. I wasn't merely saved by grace. It changed me. Now that I know who I am and whose I am, I walk with a holy certainty. I no longer doubt my sufficiency because it is rooted in Christ. I am aware that I am being observed by others who need to see if it is real. I am aware of my obligations to help others find healing.

To the woman still walking through your valley. Keep going. Don't despise your process. The next chapter of your life, which God is still currently writing, will be worth the wait. You are not forgotten. You haven't gone too far, you are being polished, you are of royal blood. As I reflect, I let go of the shame, the guilt, the should-haves and the what-ifs. I welcome the splendor of God who never gave up on me, the beauty of this instant, and the promise of tomorrow.

I carry my story like a banner, not a burden. It's my triumph, not just my past. And each page demonstrates that God is dependable, that healing is possible, and that wounded girls can grow into strong, independent women. So, I'll keep walking, not with a limp of pain but with a stride of purpose. Because the crown I wear is a sign for others, not just for me. A reminder that God is still able to heal. God continues to raise His women up from the pit. Indeed, God still crowns His daughters in glory.

Reflections

'Now if we are children, then we are heirs—heirs of God and co-heirs with Christ.' - Romans 8:17

In this chapter we discover how God's love meets us in our unique pain and lifts us into His promise. No matter how deep the wound, His grace goes deeper. Each chapter reveals a new layer of healing, identity, and purpose. God doesn't just patch us up – He makes us new. He redeems every scar, every silence, every shadow. We are not forgotten. We are not forsaken. We are seen, chosen, and called.

When we surrender the broken pieces of our past to Him, He doesn't discard them – He displays His glory through them. He shines through our cracks, providing what the enemy tried to bury, God is destined to bloom.

I want to invite you to lay down shame and pick up strength. Stop hiding and start healing. I invite you to walk boldly into the identity Christ died to give you. Your past no longer holds the pen – God does. And he is still writing.

CHAPTER 10

Purpose in the Pressing

P urpose doesn't always feel like a mountain-top experience, it often feels like a pressing. A crushing. A weight you didn't ask to carry. But it is in that pressing the oil begins to flow. I found my calling in suffering, not in a castle. I discovered it in the difficult secret locations. Where only God could see me. There, He muttered facts that served as my souls anchors. It was there He turned agony into assignment.

My destiny was irrigated by every tear I cried. A greater compassion was revealed with every heartbreak. And every "no" I heard from people was merely a way for God to say "yes" in a bigger way. I learned to look for the no's because I knew God was up to something in my life.

Why me? I used to question myself (and God for that matter). However, I now realize that God trusted me with this suffering because He knew I would utilize it for good. When I went through the domestic violence it made me see that I was not the only person going through this. That is where Restoring Inner Peace and Self-Esteem Inc. was birthed. And the work I did in the shelters. Being in that battered woman's shelter opened my eyes to a lot about what women go through, the needs they have when trying to escape that life and the reasons why some women stay. I decided I want to help the women who have escaped the cycle of abuse and want to start a new life. I want to provide them with resources and training on how to support themselves.

After being raped by my ex-husband co-worker I was afraid and did not know what to do. I was a civilian on a military base and he was active duty military. They seemed to believe his side of the story and protected him. The very next week my cousin was beaten and was dying. Because I chose to go be with my family while he was on life support the Navy decided I must have not taken the rape serious because I didn't keep the appointment they had set up for me with to discuss it further. Because I was alone and not taken serious I decided to give back to rape victims. I became a volunteer as a rape crisis counselor where I would meet rape victims at the hospital for their exam. I wanted to be the person there for them that believed and supported them.

These are just a few things that God saw my faithfulness in only what He could do. God saw that I wouldn't waste it, He knew that He could trust me. Would I chose to go through all these things again? I probably wouldn't but I can say they were things that made me a stronger person. They were things that God can use to help others.

God was aware that I would emerge from the ashes and aid in the reconstruction of others. The pressing is the only way to get the experience, it can't be taught, only birthed through brokenness. Even, if you are still mending, it offers you the ability to carry others, love deeply, and proclaim life.

When God presses you, He is not punishing you, He is preparing your voice and your vessel. You then become a carrier of oil that cannot be brought or faked. I's holy and costly. I now realize that God developed me in the same places I prayed He would save me from. Instead of being rejected, I was purified, not obliterated, but elevated in Him. And, in me every devasting experience He was creating something eternal in me.

 If you are in the pressing, don't run from it, stay right there. That suffering has a purpose. The valley contains vision. That grind has its glory. And when the oil starts flowing it will bless everyone that is connected to you. The oil is not just for you to enjoy but God will use it to change lives and set people free from bondage. Be careful not to waste the oil either.

You were not called to comfortable – you are called to carry. And what you carry is powerful. It's your testimony. It's your legacy. Is the fragrance of life fully surrendered to God. So keep going woman of God. Your oil will arrive soon. And heaven will rejoice as it flows in you, the hearts of people will mend, and chains will be broken. Because in the pressing, your true purpose is born.

Reflection

'For our light and momentary troubles are achieving for us an eternal glory...' - 2 Corinthians 4:17

In this chapter it was reminder that the pressure, the resistance, and the "hard parts" aren't punishments but important parts of our trip. In this chapter it didn't simply talk about going through terrible times; it changed the way we think about them by saying they are what make us who we need to be to live the life God is calling us to.

The lesson was clear: hard times take away what isn't needed and make what is needed stronger. Our goals and callings go through a refining stage, just the way grapes are squeezed to make wine. It's not easy and might be messy, but without the pressing, nothing changes. This made me think now how when I thought I was failing. In actuality, those were the times that made me stronger, more creative, and more clear-headed.

There is one thing that is pretty clear the pressing is connected to purpose. The pressing seems useless when we forget why we started. But if we remember our "why," the pressure turns into fuel instead of a burden. It made me think about how the moments I felt the most down in how my life was going was when I forgot about the people I would soon help.

During the pressing season, we learn the habits and ways of thinking that can help us get the gift we want. If we don't get ready, we might get the chance but not be able to handle it. I look at other areas of my life it's so tempting to want to be successful right away, but this made me realize that quick success isn't always possible.

Another important point was the admonition to trust God, the process, and the broader vision during hard times. It forced me to adjust my perspective from "Why is this happening to me?" to "What is this teaching me?" That simple change in perspective changes problems into chances to grow. And I allowed that growth in my life.

In the end, I pray that Purpose in Pressing helped you want to accept the times that seem heavy instead of fighting them. The weight will mold you, the resistance will strengthen you, and the pain is getting you ready to make a bigger difference. The pressure isn't the end; it's the only way to get to the promise.

CHAPTER 11

Divine Identity

There's no greater revelation than discovering who you are in Christ. For years, I lived according to what others said about me – too broken, too fat, too much, too shy, or not enough. But then God whispered the truth that changed my whole life. He said to me "you are mine". This changed the way I began to view myself. Before I called Him Father He called me beloved daughter. I saw rejection, but He saw royalty. I attempted to hide my scars in shame, looking for my identity. However, identity is disclosed rather than earned. And God revealed mine in the ruins.

I am not what I have gone through and neither are you. I am not what life attempted to name me. I've been called and chosen, I am fearfully and wonderfully made.

Handcrafted for the Master's use. Nothing can take me away from His love because my name is engraved on the palm of His hand,

Everything changes once you know who you are. You stop trying to fit into areas that God hasn't called you to. You quit pursuing those who don't value you. You begin to walk and talk authoritatively over your life. You begin to walk like the queen you are. And live according to the plans God has for your life. The enemy's greatest fear is a woman who knows her identity because you are a force to be reckoned with. Because she is difficult to shake. When life throws her a curveball, she doesn't break. When audiences doesn't applaud, she doesn't back down. She stands firm not in pride, but in purpose.

When your anchor is your divine identity, when storms rage, it keeps you steady. When the world forgets, it serves as a reminder of your value. Even when the ground beneath you changes, it keeps you firmly planted in grace. I used to strive to become someone other than who God created me to be due to trying to please others. Now I rest in who I am. I am a masterpiece, uniquely created for a specific purpose. God cherishes me for who He created me to be. His glory is reflected upon me. Furthermore, that identity cannot be sold, stolen or destroyed.

If you have forgotten who you are, go back to the Word of God. You are the product of God's mercy, not the sum of your mistakes. You were hand-picked not ignored. And you were never meant to blend in – you were born to stand out. Your divine identity is this: a woman who is filled with destiny, dresses with dignity, and crown with courage, now walk in it. Take ownership of it and live it. Because when you embrace who God says you are, the world can no longer define you – and hell can no longer defeat you.

Reflections

'But you are a chosen people, a royal priesthood...' - 1 Peter 2:9

After writing this chapter, I felt like I was given a mirror when I reread Divine Identity—not one that shows how the world sees me, but one that shows how God has always seen me. I hope this chapter was not just words to you; I pray that it was a coming back to yourself after times when life, pain, and other people's views tried to change your name but God did not allow that to happen.

The main idea of the chapter was the fact that identity is given, not earned, made up, or based on conditions. It's impossible to change who you are when it comes from God, even when everything else in your life seems to be coming apart. The truth hit even harder when I was honest about my problems, like when I felt seen, unworthy, or defined by my wounds. Our crown may crack, but it's never taken away, God is will use it for His glory.

One of the most important things I learned was that hard

times don't make us less valuable in God's eyes. Betrayals, losses, and mistakes in life can make us question who we are, but they don't change how God made us. It's very easy to believe the words that other people have said about us, like "too much," "not enough," "broken," or "unqualified." That's not true, though. Divine Identity tells us the truth: we are chosen, loved, anointed, and prepared.

CHAPTER 12

Don't Hide the Cracks

Looking back at all the times I tried to hide the cracks seemed at the time the right thing to do. I thought the goal was to be flawless, to appear put together, untouched by pain and unshaken by trauma. But now I see the cracks was never the problem. They were the places where the light got in.

Every wound, scar and crack in my spirit serves as a portal for the splendor of God. He considered what I thought shameful to be sacred. He took my brokenness and made it a source of inspiration for others. God gave me a voice while life attempted to silence me. God poured forth His light, till it radiated out of my entire essence in the crevices where the enemy attempted to harm me. My suffering became my platform, and the shattered vessel became a lamp.

This journey taught me that strength isn't in pretending nothing hurts. Strength is in surrender. Strength is letting God shine through the shattered pieces we wrongfully think disqualifies us. Give everything to God and watch Him shine through your cracks.

I used to believe that the goal was to return to my pre-trauma self. However, I discovered that I never want to return to that person. Because this kind of glory was unknown to me before the breaking. God is an expert in fixing broken things. He enjoys repairing the broken, not throwing them away. He fills the gaps with Himself rather than trying to hide them. And when His light floods those places you don't just survive you shine.

There is beauty in brokenness. Not because the suffering is beautiful. But I found that God intervened and change it to be something that made me need Him. He used what was intended for evil to illuminate my path of healing. You are being positioned, if you feel broken, you are in the place where God's light can shine in. You will get in position to carry honor, positioned to serve as a vessel, reflecting God's glory. I now hold my head up high not because I'm complete in the eyes of the world, but because I am radiant in the eyes of God. His light is shining through the crevices and I am not longer ashamed.

I am a living walking example that broken doesn't equate to be buried. "Bright" signifies "broken."

Reflections

'But we have this treasure in jars of clay...' - 2 Corinthians 4:6-7

I wanted this chapter to show my readers that challenges in life are both painful and hopeful at the same time. In this chapter my story doesn't hide the cracks that were there because of things like domestic violence, lying, loss, and the constant hits that life gave me. In this chapter I didn't let the cracks have the last word either. Instead, I wanted show everyone the truth of a loving God: it's in those cracks that God's light shines through, so embrace them.

I wanted this chapter to have you imagine yourself sitting in a dark room and watching sunshine come in through a broken window. The light didn't try to avoid the damage; it used it as a way in. There are real marks left behind. and I wanted to honor that fact without making it sound better. I wanted you see how God can use something that was meant to hurt you to heal you and show His glory.

The most important lesson is that the cracks are not signs of shameful weakness that need to be hidden, but signs of grace and survival. In fact, this chapter changes the whole meaning of them: the cracks show that you've been through the fire, but they're also the places where God's presence is clearest. They might not make it possible to see the light as well without them. I pray that you understanding this fact makes you feel both humble and free.

The truth that light doesn't need to be perfect to shine— it just needs a way in. Those gaps are often made by our wounds. Light Through the Cracks makes us question the idea that God can only use us when we're "healed" or "whole." The damage doesn't stop God's light; it passes through it and is a light that others see as something beautiful..

This part also shows how testimony can save people. You give other people permission to see their own cracks when you let them see yours. And when they see the light coming through yours, it makes them want to believe that God can use their sadness to make something beautiful. This makes the chapter more than just personal; it's also a mission that God has placed on my life to help others.

As time went on and people healed, the cracks that felt like open wounds turned into ways for strength, knowledge, and kindness to flow outward toward others. God is the only one who can change things like that— taking something that was meant to quiet you and turning it into a light that leads others to Him.

My prayer is that this chapter shows how powerful God's healing is. To remember that His light can reach all damage, no matter how deep it goes. When it does, it doesn't just light up our lives; it pours out of us to help others find their way. The cracks are still there, but they're not just marks of pain anymore; they're signs of honor. We should remember that fact for the rest of our lives.

CHAPTER 13

Royal Redemption

Redemption doesn't always come with trumpets and parades. Sometimes, it looks like finally sleeping through the nights without fear of your life being taken. Sometimes, it's laughing without guilt. Sometimes it's simply waking up and choosing to live.

Redemption was a slow process for me. It was a sacred reclaiming of all the aspects of myself that I believed was lost. My voice. My ideals. My worth. And God returned it all, piece by piece, but this time with a crown of glory and a crown of grace. Shame was once a veil I wore. Now I wear royalty like a robe. I once thought that I was too wounded, to forgotten, and too far for gone as stated before. But my story was rewritten by redemption. A declaration of victory replaced what had been a murmur of failure. God restored me, not just saved me. He called me back into my role of a vessel not a victim. Not as a footnote but as a front-line warrior. I don't just walk with freedom – I walk with fire.

Redemption indicated that nothing was thrown away. The time, the trauma, and the tears. All of it was, used by God to mold me into a bold vessel. A woman who is aware of her identity and her place in life. I walk differently now, I walk with favor rather than fear. My purpose now defines me, not my history.

What about my crown? It's for demonstrating the grace of God not for decorating. To all the women who are still waiting in quiet for your change. Know that there is hope for atonement. Restoration is still possible. And there is more to your story. You will meet the same God who met me among my wreckage.

This is what royal redemption looks like, a woman who has survived the fire but does not smell like smoke. An oil-carrying woman who has been crushed. A woman who decided to rise despite having every incentive to give up. That woman is me, that woman is you too. Despite your broken beginnings you are beautiful. Despite having experienced hell, you were created for heavenly purposes.

God see you, even though you may feel invisible, and He is asking you to rise up.

Reflection

'I will restore to you the years that the locust has eaten...'
- Joel 2:25

When you finish reading Royal Redemption, I wanted you to take a deep breath, like when you take that breath after a storm and realize you made it through. Yes, God is still in the business of giving everything back, no matter how much was lost. This chapter is a success song.

It was so clear to me how repair can look, not just bits and pieces, but the whole thing. God didn't just fix the things that were broken in my life; He made them better, more beautiful, and full of more value than they were before. It was true that they lost. The scars are still there. But the crown does too, and now it shines with the gold of God's honor.

Hope is what this part is all about. I am grateful that God gave me back my identity, my happiness, my sense of worth, and even dreams I thought were lost forever. He gave me back relationships, chances, and happiness in ways that I couldn't have planned on my own. This kind of healing shows that God not only heals, but also increases.

CHAPTER 14

Crowning Moments

Every woman has a turning point in her life when the crown takes on a spiritual significance. It has nothing to do with jewelry or fame. It's about the fate and identity finally catching up. It involves walking into what heaven spoke long before the earth took notice. I felt unworthy for years. The weight of my past made me believe I wasn't qualified to wear anything royal. And that I had to live life as it was presented to me. However, God reminded me that perfection does not earn one a crown. It is a testament to His promises. You have been chosen despite what tried to break you.

I recall when it finally clicked. I already had a title, why be disappointed when you didn't get the title from man. So this helps me when I stepped out of my comfort zone and try new things. I am not disappointed that I did not win what man was handing out. The winning comes with me growing in new experiences. Stepping out of my comfort zone has been a hinderance for me before, so now I am just doing things afraid. I am not worried about being rejected again because I know who I am in Christ and He is what matters. I just like doing things I have never done before. Even in the pageant Ms. Senior Jacksonville 2025 I was just in the crowning moment didn't happen on the stage. It happened in my spirit. It happened the day I forgave. The day I let go. The day that heaven placed the crown I had been fighting to deserve, gently on my head.

It takes time to become a queen. Every decision we make to rise above, love more deeply, and speak truth even when our voice shakes. We are readjusting our crown each time we say "yes" to God and "no" to fear. It's not just how you walk, it's about how you carry others with you. True queens don't just wear crowns – they complete rather than compete. They create rather than destroy.

My crowning moment was a holy declaration rather than just a selfish triumph. "This woman has survived the fire and is still radiant" despite being broken. She continues to believe. She stands despite having every motive to hide.

Your crowing moment is coming. It may not look like what you expect, but it will feel like peace. You'll feel like you belong. It will resemble a father's embrace who has never forgotten your name. With that being said, walk with courage, heart full and head high. Queen reposition your crown when needed and continue on. Because no one can take away what God has placed on you. And when you wear it beautifully, you serve as a reminder to the world of what grace-encased grandeur looks like.

Reflection

'Blessed is the one who perseveres under trial because, having stood the test...' - James 1:12

The chapter Crowning Moments is full of happiness. At this point in the story, all the lines of pain, faith, persistence, and hope come together, and God's presence can't be denied. I wanted this chapter to show the turning point every woman goes through, when God steps in and changes everything.

My crowning moment didn't happen because of perfect circumstances or a perfect trip. It happened when I least expected it but needed it the most: in the middle of the mess. What a wonderful God we have! He doesn't wait for us to be perfect before He meets us where we are and gives us His favor, love, and purpose.

I wanted one of the most powerful things about this chapter to be how I showed that a crowning moment isn't always big in the eyes of everyone else. Sometimes it's quiet—a change in your heart, a deep sense that God has moved on. Sometimes it's big and public—a big step forward, an answer you've been waiting for, or a real blessing that leaves you speechless. It changes you no matter what form it takes.

Also, I wanted it to be clear that these events are not by chance. They are divine plans that God timed just right, and they often happen during times we thought were barren. It takes time, effort, and patience to get ready to wear the crown. When it is finally put on, we understand that the journey was worth it because it made us ready.

I realized that times of crowning often come after moments of surrender. God's power shows up in ways we couldn't have planned when we let go of our plans, our pride, and our schedule. God doesn't just fix us when we trust Him with our flaws; He also makes us better.

CHAPTER 15

The Final Flourish

This is not the end of my story – it's the beginning of yours. Because everything I've walked through wasn't just for me. It was for every woman who needs to know that survival is just the first step, flourishing is your destiny.

I shine now where I was once buried. I used to be silent, but now I speak. I used to be broken, but now I'm the one that God uses to give people hope. You see, I was brought through by God, not merely out. Through the valley, through the shame, through the stillness and through the flames. On the other side I discovered meaning in addition to healing. This book is more than a testimony. It's a torch. And, now I'm handing it to you. Light your way. Let it serve as a reminder that you still have a voice. Your path is holy. Additionally, your crown is ready and waiting on you.

Not only do we conquer, but we also build after conquering. We construct bridges for other people to cross. We build altars of remembrance. We build legacy. What tried to destroy me did not win. What tried to steal my voice didn't succeed. I'm still here standing stronger than before. I am whole. I belong to Christ. Let your life reflect heaven's glory. Be a living example of courage, redemption, and divine identity.

As I lay down my pen, I lift up praise to the One who kept me. To the One who crowned me. To the One who turned my pain into purpose and my brokenness into light. I pray this last chapter opens your heart rather than be just a closing of a book. Accept your calling. Walk into your purpose with courage. Live as the woman of God you were created to be. You are the splendor and a triumphant daughter of the King of Kings.

Reflection

'He who began a good work in you will carry it on to completion...' - Philippians 1:6

The Final Flourish is the perfect ending to a trip that was full of loss, gain, and pain. This chapter tells us that even though the crown was broken, it has been fixed and now has the beauty that can only come from God's hand on it. This flourish isn't about going back to the person you were before the storms; it's about becoming the person you've become because of them.

The weight of everything that led to this point was heavy. The pressing, breaking, honing, and waiting. Everything was important at this time. The last touch is when you look at the fabric from the front instead of the back, where the threads are all tangled. You understand that God wasn't just fixing you; He was also making a beauty.

I wanted it to be clear that God always finishes what He starts. There isn't a rushed finish or a neat bow on top of a messy story in the flourish. It's an exclamation point from God, a sign of how faithful and skilled He is in your life. Each scar has turned into something strong. There are seeds of joy that have grown from every tear. Every loss has made room for a gain that is even bigger.

ABOUT THE AUTHOR

Dr. Cheryl Kehl is a devoted wife, mother, grandmother, and great-grandmother who lives a life of service, strength, and spiritual purpose. A veteran of both the United States Navy and United States Air Force, she brings the same courage and discipline from her military service into her ministry work today.

Dr. Kehl is a full-time minister, Certified Master Life Coach, domestic violence coach and advocate, and licensed travel agent. Her powerful testimony as a thriver—not just a survivor—of domestic violence has become a beacon of hope for women seeking healing and restoration. With a heart for mentoring, she equips women to rise from the ashes of pain and walk boldly in their divine purpose.

An Amazon bestselling author and dynamic speaker, Dr. Kehl has co-authored seven transformative book projects and released two devotionals available on Amazon. She also hosted the inspirational Christian TV talk show *Walking in Greatness*, where she shared stories of faith,

triumph, and purpose. If this has blessed you email me and share at cherylkehl@yahoo.com.

Made in the USA
Columbia, SC
11 September 2025

62079775R00043